AF604602

JOHN LESLEY

# WEDGE-TAILED EAGLE

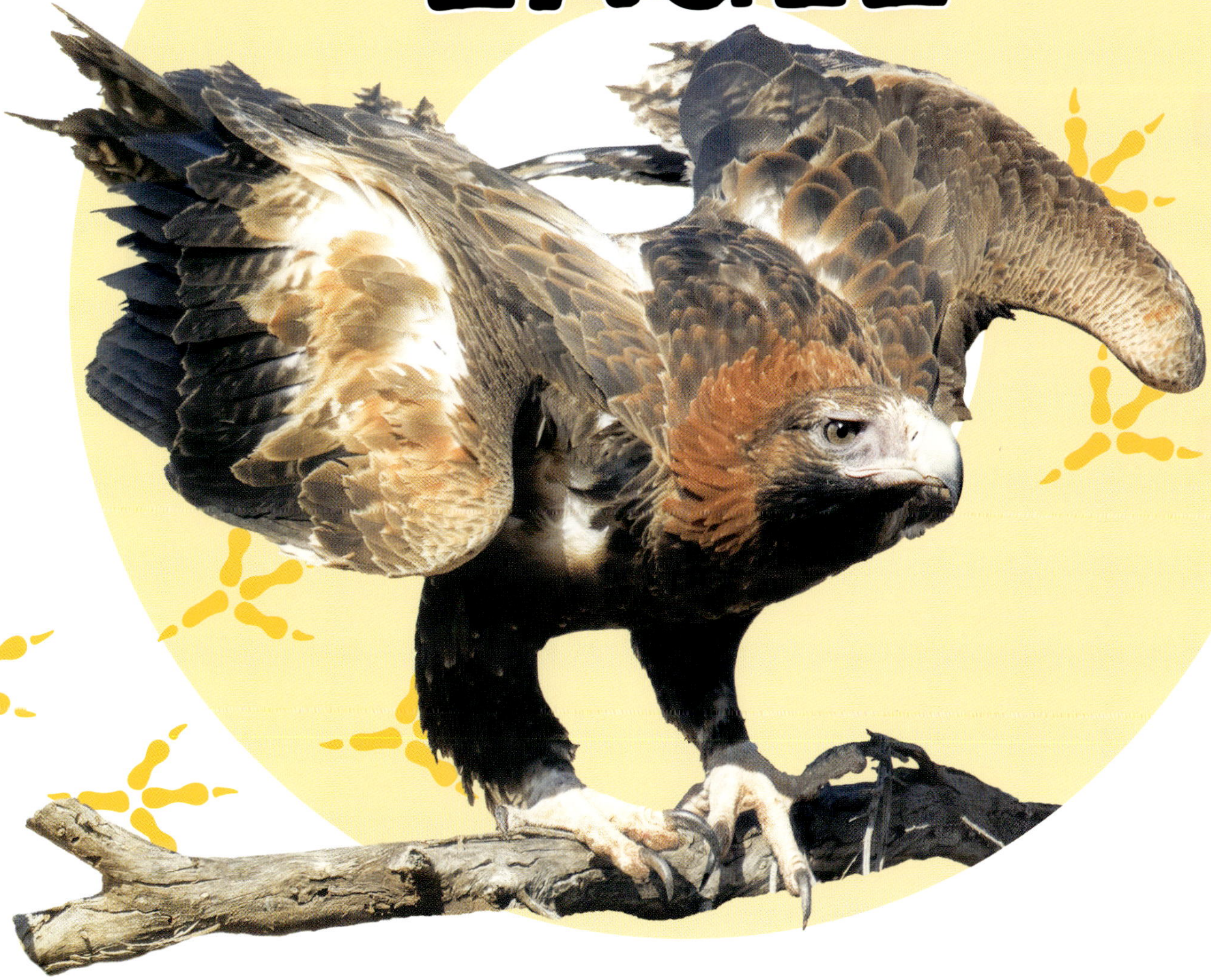

First Published 2024 by
Redback Publishing
Suite 6, 13a Narabang Way,
Belrose NSW 2085
Australia

www.redbackpublishing.com
info@redbackpublishing.com

© Redback Publishing 2024

ISBN 978-1-761400-70-4

All rights reserved. No part of this publication may be reproduced in any form or by any means (including photocopying or storing it in any medium by electronic means and whether or not transiently or incidentally to some other use of this publication) without the written permission of the copyright owner. Applications for the copyright owner's written permission should be addressed to the publisher.

Author: John Lesley
Editor: Caroline Thomas
Design: Redback Publishing

A catalogue record for this book is available from the National Library of Australia

Original illustrations © Redback Publishing 2024
Originated by Redback Publishing

Acknowledgements
Abbreviations: l—left, r—right, b—bottom, t—top, c—centre, m—middle
We would like to thank the following for permission to reproduce photographs: (Images © shutterstock) pg8tr Ed Dunens, CC BY 2.0 <https://creativecommons.org/licenses/by/2.0>, via Wikimedia Commons, pg10br fir0002 flagstaffotos [at] gmail.com, Canon 5D III + Canon 400mm f/5.6 L, GFDL 1.2 <http://www.gnu.org/licenses/old-licenses/fdl-1.2.html>, via Wikimedia Commons, pg15c Atwoxby, CC BY-SA 4.0 <https://creativecommons.org/licenses/by-sa/4.0>, via Wikimedia Commons, pg15tr Atwoxby, CC BY-SA 4.0 <https://creativecommons.org/licenses/by-sa/4.0>, via Wikimedia Commons, pg18tr James Niland, CC BY 2.0 <https://creativecommons.org/licenses/by/2.0>, via Wikimedia Commons, pg26bl Alisperic, Creative Commons Attribution-Share Alike 4.0 International via Wikipedia Commons, pg26br Nils Versemann/Shutterstock.com, pg27ml Douglas Clif/Shutterstock.com, pg27br Rose MarinelliShutterstock.com

Disclaimer
Every effort has been made to contact copyright holders of any material reproduced in this book. Any omissions will be rectified in subsequent printings if notice is given to the publisher.

# CONTENTS


What is a Wedge-tailed Eagle? 4
Raptors 6
Wedge-tailed Eagle Basic Facts 8
Wedge-tailed Eagle Body 10
'Eagle-Eyed' 12
Wedge-tailed Eagle Life Cycle 14
Wedge-tailed Eagle Habitats 16
What They Eat 18
Threats to the Wedge-tailed Eagle 20
Wedge-tailed Eagles and People 22
Where to See a Wedge-tailed Eagle 24
Wedge-tailed Eagles as Symbols 26
Eagles of the World 28
Sorting Animals into Groups 30
Glossary 32
Index 32

# WHAT IS A WEDGE-TAILED EAGLE?

In the Australian Outback, the wedge-tailed eagle is the dominant predator in the skies. Even on land, a healthy, fully grown wedge-tailed eagle is a match for any animal predator that might be foolish enough to try to attack it.

The magnificent wedge-tailed eagle is rare in urban areas, so most people in Australia will never see one in the wild.

In comparison with other eagles of the world, the wedge-tailed eagle is not the biggest, but it does rank highly amongst them in wingspan, height and weight.

Many Indigenous Australian stories include wedge-tailed eagles. Their strength and intelligence make them creatures of great importance.

# RAPTORS

Wedge-tailed eagles belong to the group of birds called raptors. This group also includes hawks, falcons, owls, vultures and buzzards. There are raptors all around the world, except in Antarctica.

White-tailed eagle
*Haliaeetus albicilla*

Raptors spot their prey from the air, then dive down to snatch the animal from the ground or from water. They may eat it on the ground, or carry the prey to a safer place where they can rip it into small chunks without fear of being attacked themselves. Australia's wedge-tailed eagles sometimes catch other birds in mid-air.

Raptors do not have teeth. Instead, they have a sharp hook on the end of their beak that is used for tearing flesh into smaller pieces which can be swallowed more easily.

The extinct dinosaur group called raptors had many features of modern eagles. However, most raptor dinosaurs grew much bigger and had teeth!

Raptors are excellent hunters and they are all carnivores. They have strong, muscular bodies and legs equipped with long, sharp talons for holding prey.

# WEDGE-TAILED EAGLE BASIC FACTS

## SCIENTIFIC NAME

The wedge-tailed eagle's scientific name is *Aquila audax*, which means 'bold, courageous eagle'. The common name 'wedge-tailed', comes from the wide, arrow or diamond shape of the tail in flight.

## SOUNDS

The adults rarely call to each other except when they are together raising chicks. They then might make a high-pitched whistling or squawking noise.

## COLOUR

Adult wedge-tailed eagles have brown to black feathers, with a few specks of cream. The chicks have white down, and the juveniles are brown, black and reddish. The beak and feet are a cream colour.

## CONSERVATION STATUS

The IUCN Red List of animal conservation status lists the wedge-tailed eagle as being of 'Least Concern'. This means that, according to their research, this eagle is not under current threat of extinction.

Despite this listing, people who live in areas where wedge-tailed eagles used to exist, now sometimes say they have not seen them in the sky for a long time.

## TASMANIA

The Tasmanian subspecies or group, *Aquila audax fleayi*, may be under threat. It is larger than its mainland cousins and could be more susceptible to loss of habitat due to human activity.

# THE WEDGE-TAILED EAGLE BODY

## SIZE AND SHAPE

Wedge-tailed eagles have a sharp, curved beak, strong claws and amazing eyesight. Their legs and claws are so strong that they can carry a dead animal that weighs as much as a cat or small dog. The legs are very long in comparison with other birds, and the claws are vicious. The eagle has four toes on each foot, three pointing forwards and one backwards. Each toe has a talon that is used by the eagle like a sharp knife.

The body is big and heavy, weighing up to about five kilograms, with females being larger than males. Wedge-tailed eagles can stand a metre high and have a wingspan of about two and a half metres.

## FLIGHT ADAPTATIONS

Wedge-tailed eagles can fly well over a kilometre high in the sky, soaring on rising air currents. This reduces the need to flap their wings, and conserves energy while searching vast distances for food.

The wings are long and narrow, a feature found in birds that soar for long periods in the air. This adaptation does have a negative impact when the eagle is on the ground in a densely wooded area.

It is harder for a bird with this wing shape to get off the ground than it is for birds such as pigeons which have wider-shaped wings. An eagle struggling to get airborne can become a target for predators.

## BOOTED EAGLES

The legs have feathers all the way down to the claws, which is unusual in birds. Because of this feature, they are sometimes called 'booted eagles', because the leg feathers make them look like they are wearing long boots.

# 'EAGLE-EYED'

Wedge-tailed eagles can see further than humans, and in more colours and better detail. They sit at the top of a tall tree, or a power pole, watching for any movement within hundreds of metres all around. When they see something they want to catch for food, they silently swoop down and kill it.

Their excellent, long-distance eyesight depends on daylight, so these eagles hunt in the daytime.

Eagles are so well-known for having remarkable eyesight, that the term 'eagle-eyed' is used for a person who never misses noticing the tiniest detail.

# WEDGE-TAILED EAGLE LIFE CYCLE

## MATING AND NESTING

Wedge-tailed eagles pair with a mate and usually stay together for more than one breeding season. They build a very large and heavy nest, sometimes up to two metres wide, high in a tree or on a cliff face. They defend their territory by chasing off other eagles or intruders.

Wedge-tailed eagle nest

## JUVENILES

Once the young leave the nest, they will stay together for a few weeks. Roadkill will attract these young eagles, and there can be a few of them all feeding at once.

Since the young do not fully mature until they are about six years old, they tend to stay in groups until they start to breed. This is when they need to move further apart and claim their own territories.

# EGGS AND CHICKS

After mating, the female lays about three eggs, but it is rare for all of them to survive once they hatch. The first chick to hatch may kill the others. This gives the survivor a very good chance of reaching adulthood. The chicks are covered in soft, white feathers called 'down'.

# FEEDING

The parents share the care of the young, but it is usually the female that sits on the eggs and feeds the chicks from food brought back to the nest by the male. She tears the food into small pieces that the chick or chicks can eat.

In the wild, wedge-tailed eagles may live for up to twenty years. In captivity, they have been known to live for up to thirty years.

# WEDGE-TAILED EAGLE HABITATS

Wedge-tailed eagles live in nearly every habitat across Australia and its offshore islands, except for in the driest deserts. They also live in the forests and grasslands of southern New Guinea.

Wedge-tailed eagles need to have a habitat with high trees or rocky cliff faces where they can perch to survey their territory and also build their nests. If tall trees are not available, a wedge-tailed eagle will use power poles or other structures made by people.

Because of their large wingspan, wedge-tailed eagles are not often found in dense rainforests. They prefer to live and hunt in open forests, grasslands and semi-arid regions. They will live near the outer parts of towns, where they prey on the rats and mice that are attracted to human rubbish.

# WHAT THEY EAT

Wedge-tailed eagles are carnivores. They hunt their prey from the air and will catch other birds mid-air. They will also eat dead animals that they see as they soar across the countryside.

Their diet includes wallabies, other marsupials, rabbits, feral puppies and kittens, lizards and occasionally insects. They do not usually eat fish.

Wedge-tailed eagles will hunt in groups to catch a large prey animal, such as a kangaroo. They rip at it until it dies, then gather around to eat.

Livestock such as lambs or chickens will be taken for food, but wedge-tailed eagles are not a major predator of these animals.

There are rare reports of wedge-tailed eagles attacking children and small pets.

Most people will only ever get to see a wild wedge-tailed eagle when they have to swerve their car around it on the road. Eagles eat roadkill and can be so intent on feeding that they barely notice a car coming. This can result in them becoming roadkill themselves.

# THREATS TO WEDGE-TAILED EAGLES

## PREDATORS

Wedge-tailed eagles have no predators in the sky, although a group of smaller birds, such as magpies and noisy miners, will try to drive an eagle away.

On the ground, a sick or unwary young eagle can be taken by a feral dog or cat, but the eagle's sharp talons will still present a danger to any attacker.

## HABITAT LOSS

The main threat to the wedge-tailed eagle is the loss of its habitat. They need tall trees for nesting, and large expanses of land in which to hunt for food.

Smaller birds, such as magpies, will try to drive an eagle away.

## POISONING

Government campaigns to kill feral dogs and cats by leaving poison baits in the wild can also kill native animals, including wedge-tailed eagles. An eagle that takes the bait, or eats an animal that has been poisoned, might also die from poisoning.

# WEDGE-TAILED EAGLES AND PEOPLE

## ROADS

Wedge-tailed eagles like to find an easy meal by eating roadkill, but they can then become road accident victims themselves.

Australia's wedge-tailed eagle is one of the largest eagles in the world, yet not many Australians know much about it. The only encounter they might ever have with this metre-high bird is likely to be when they suddenly come upon one in the middle of the road, and have to break the car suddenly to avoid an accident.

## SHOOTING

In the past, farmers were allowed to shoot and poison wedge-tailed eagles to stop lambs from being attacked and eaten. The number of lambs killed was probably very low, but wedge-tailed eagles are now protected by law.

## RABBITS

Although feral rabbits are a pest throughout Australia, their introduction into the Outback has been good for the wedge-tailed eagle. Rabbits make up a large part of an eagle's diet and have contributed to the continued existence of the wedge-tailed eagle.

## EAGLES AND TECHNOLOGY

Wedge-tailed eagles guard their territory, both on the ground and high up in the sky. They will chase off other eagles, but will also angrily attack drones and hang gliders. Wind turbines are a modern threat to wedge-tailed eagles, as are power lines that cause death through electrocution.

# WHERE TO SEE WEDGE-TAILED EAGLES

## THE OUTBACK

Eagles are not common or easy to find in the wild. They soar so high in the sky that they look like black dots. On the ground, a breeding pair has a territory that can be a kilometre wide, so finding them is difficult.

Any disruption to their territory by human activities could make a breeding pair leave their nest and move away.

If you are lucky and patient, you might see one flying low, or perching on a tree. A wedge-tailed eagle that finds you in its territory might fly over you to check out what you are and what you are doing. They will be high up and silent, so you might not even notice them doing this.

## ZOOS

Zoos often train a wedge-tailed eagle with methods that have been used by falconers for thousands of years. This involves raising a bird from when it is a chick and using food as a way to communicate what the handler wants the eagle to do.

Wedge-tailed eagles are smart and observant, so a trained, tame eagle can put on a fascinating show for the public.

These eagles are bred in captivity and would probably find survival in the wild a challenge because of being raised by humans.

# WEDGE-TAILED EAGLES AS SYMBOLS

For thousands of years, people have chosen eagles as mascots and as symbols of bravery and strength. In Australia today, the wedge-tailed eagle is a popular choice as a logo, mascot or emblem.

An image of the wedge-tailed eagle appears on the Australian Defence Force ensign, where it represents the Royal Australian Air Force (RAAF).

La Trobe University in Victoria has a wedge-tailed eagle holding a scroll as its brandmark.

The wedge-tailed eagle is the bird emblem of the Northern Territory, and it also appears atop their Coat of Arms.

Northern Territory Coat of Arms

The RAAF Wedgetail aircraft are named after the wedge-tailed eagle.

The NSW Police Force has a flying wedge-tailed eagle as part of its emblem.

# EAGLES OF THE WORLD

Steller's Sea-Eagle
Haliaeetus pelagicus
(Northeast Asia)
White-Tailed Eagle
Haliaeetus albicilla
(Northern Europe
and Asia)
Philippine Eagle
Pithecophaga jefferyi
(Philippines)
AFRICAN FISH EAGLE
Icthyophaga vocifer
(Africa)
4K UHD
00:35:02

# SORTING ANIMALS INTO GROUPS

Biologists divide all living things around the world into groups. They call this process classification.

The two basic groups of animals are called:

**VERTEBRATES**

Vertebrates have a backbone

**INVERTEBRATES**

Invertebrates do not have a backbone

Vertebrates are further divided into five groups called classes. Wedge-tailed eagles are birds and belong in the class called Aves.

# GLOSSARY

**adaptation** change in a living thing to make it better able to survive

**airborne** being in the air

**carnivore** animal that only eats meat

**categorise** sort into categories or groups

**down** soft, fluffy feathers

**ensigns** official flags of the Australian Defence Force or of government services

**formidable** powerful and frightening

**predator** animal that hunts and eats other animals

**prey** animal that is hunted and eaten by another animal

**roadkill** dead animals that have been hit by cars on roads

**soar** fly using rising air currents

**specks** small spots

**survey (verb)** check on an area

**susceptible** could be harmed by

**talon** sharp, long claw

**wingspan** width of wings when spread out

# INDEX


booted eagles 11
chicks 8, 9, 15, 25
lambs 19, 22
lifespan 15
nests 14, 15, 17, 20, 24
New Guinea 16
Outback 4, 23, 24
poison 21, 22
predators 4, 11, 19, 20, 32
roadkill 14, 19, 22, 32
talons 7, 10, 11, 20, 32
Tasmania 9
territory 14, 16, 17, 23, 24
wings 4, 10, 11, 17, 32
zoos 25